CW01080208

THE APPROPRIATE
COUNTRY

THE APPROPRIATE
COUNTRY

Amanda Sewell

waterloo press

First published in 2001
by Waterloo Press (Hove),
51 Waterloo Street, Hove,
East Sussex, BN3 1AH

Typesetting by Tristan Green Design
Printed in Great Britain by Antony Rowe Ltd.
Chippenham, Wiltshire

Amanda Sewell is hereby identified as author of this
work in accordance with Section 77 of the Copyright,
Designs and Patents Act, 1988

A CIP record for this book is available
from the British Library

ISBN 1-902-731-11-5

for my son Alexander with love

Contents

Acknowledgments

I should like to thank the magazines in which some of these poems first appeared: *Eratica, Foolscap, The Listener, London Magazine, Nineties Poetry, Plain Poetry, Quadrant and Twentieth Century.*

'In The Hotel Wilson, Ghent', was runner-up in the All-Sussex Downlands Poetry competition, 1981.

I'd also like to thank my husband, Nicholas Sewell, for his love, encouragement and support; my friend and editor, Simon Jenner, for his inspired suggestions, and Oliver Tatum for some creative pruning; Judith Burns, for help with the MSS, and Ralph Davis for his interest.

We acknowledge grateful thanks to South-East Arts for their assistance.

That's the appropriate country; there, man's thought
      Rarer, intenser,
    Self-gathered for an outbreak, as it ought,
      Chafes in the censer.

'A Grammarian's Funeral' *Robert Browning*

Marine Parade

Just before the summer
scaffolding is taken out
like long, slim pencils,
and placed against
the stucco buildings,
this sea-front, lavishly-lit
as a filmset, is poised
on this late, spring day.
to be applauded. Yet
no-one is here. The beach
is empty. A wide, blonde
welcome mat. Sea-washed,
waiting for visitors.

Brightonia

The sea is moving marble
in a Westall print.

Permed, grey waves
gripped by iron piers.

White Regency facades,
are man-made cliffs,

as terraced houses
stream like ceiling wax,

or painted toes,
in red-bricked rows,

where seagulls nest.
An *operafest* of stereophonic crows.

Cuckmere Haven

Where the river meets
the sea, as if a snake
had looped over the large
flat dish of estuary, swans
come in to land, feet-first,
over brisk, choppy water.

Kestrels stall in the thermals
above the saltmarshes, where
scant trees are blown into
question marks, and cottages cling
to the hulls of white ocean-liners:
the Seven Sisters in full sail.

Over the downland turf, past
the ice-white summer sheep,
we climb higher to the *Belle Tout*
lighthouse, and the darker paths
that lead up to the edge of cliffs,
and on to Beachy Head.

Mot Juste

Not being able to find a pen that would write,
found me searching
in that old pencil-box with its heavy lid
of varnished Alpine flowers.

From within this wooden little coffin,
crammed with childhood: one acid pencil,
green as a boiled sweet, had my name
engraved upon it like an obituary.

Battlefields

'I hear an army'
James Joyce

Driving through France, aged five,
with my parents: young, pre-divorce, still alive,
I heard marching feet and guns echo down
the dark corridors of flat roads near Verdun.

Their slack marriage, about to crack, my father
put on the brakes, got out, and looked
into the distance, like a man dropping
through clear air turbulence into the void.

All they heard was the swish-swish of poplars.
No tractor, cow-slow, with its heavy load,
was following their '50s Ford.
They barely spoke, alone on that road,

as their solitary child, still at the Clark's san-
dals
stage, played, hands clasped over ears
to hold out the noise. Close to the border
now, my father drove all night.

They talked in softer whispers then,
of poppy fields that said: remember the dead.

Concerning the Spiritual in
Motherhood

With thanks to A. Alvarez

My mother and I
are like two geisha girls

sipping our identical tea
in that camomile room of hers...

Sunday morning,
those exquisite hands unfold,

where green light wells
from plants, in that faint hush

of oatmeal dragons and faded velvets.

I leave to take a blue bath
of marigold petals,
wishing Kandinsky would appear,
glossy as a red plum, with his white teeth
sinking into the granular taste of summer,
at a tournament between
the red oval and the blue rider.

Outside the light
merges into damp millet.

My mother and I
rearrange the faded peonies.

[6]

Exploring the Arctic

Arctic Circle.
It maps the space between us:
long-distance calls
across the Greenland Sea. AT&T.

Polar regions apart.
Airlines looping among longitudes,
along Amundsen's route,
through the Bering Strait

to the North Pole's heart.
Par avion on the envelope,
stamped and franked
from the air are iced-over rivers,

etched like the traces
of an ice-skater's boot. Dreadful
uncharted territories, where even
explorers of the heart don't tread.

We fly as far as the Beaufort Sea,
frozen like the overwintering ships
sailed by Franklin, Ross and Parry.
Boxed in ice. Minus zero degrees.

Seattle 1

The trees here are opening up
like cape gooseberries
shedding their papery, cocktail-umbrella
leaves into the cold Pacific Northwest air.
Emerald City. No longer green -
but red, amber and tangerine.
I love this city; I'm drinking *latte*,
and I'm having a really nice day.

Flying to Alaska

From my window seat
on this Boeing 737
flight to Anchorage
I can see, looking down,
remote outcrops
of tiny, liminal communities
with their palette of green, amber and brown.

We're flying over
Vancouver Island now,
into brilliant sunshine, snowy mountains
in the distance, and a last wedge of blue sky
before we reach Alaska, when
all becomes white,
impenetrable cloud, and this late October
fin de saison day turns suddenly into night.

Seattle II

After a ten-hour flight,
jet-lagged and coffeed-up
I take my first American
power shower,
and wash British grime
away. This is an ephiphany,
an iconographic moment
of lovers' trysts, *film noir,*
Hitchcock and psychosis.
This is America.
The large, white towels are king-sized
and I feel I'm in the movies.

Barrow

North Alaska

Today the sky is whiter than snow.
The sun rises: red as *Bac n' Pieces*
in the Arctic Coastal Trading Store
at the corner of Ankovah Street, where
the frozen ocean, solid as Pompeii,
is a tableau of *crème de menthe* green:
a freeze-frame, repeated again and again.

Black as bullets, cartoonish snow-mobiles,
batman out of this frozen Gotham,
on to the tundra, with its skating-rink ice,
as buttermilk polar bears with curranty eyes,
gather under the gothic arches of Bowhead
whale jaw-bones: famished; framed,
gigantic, mythic ghosts: immense; immane.

The Northern lights weave coloured
curtains in the sky. Browerville's a bracelet
lit by stars. Huskies in their dog lots
bark all night - hushed by snow drifts
down the streets. Upturned, a Chevy
lies abandoned in the snow:
shouldering the blows of the Arctic wind.

Teolo

There are 12 of us. All holed up.
 In this hotel. End of season.
With jack-in-the-box thunderstorms
over the hills. State-of-the-art
telephones. And the long table at night
spread out like the Last Supper.

By day, we walk the Euganeum Hills,
cracking walnuts under foot:
(those curled up foetuses inside),
past the dark glamour of grapes
hidden in vineyards. Giorgione's

landscape of cypress and Italian
élan vital. Chestnuts and apricots
fall at our feet. Terrazzos and verandahs
spiral in pink. We drink wine
and eat bread, while you sit, Christ-like,
at the head of our table.

Chekhov Visits Bagara

This corner of Queensland, near the coast,
has burning fields of sugar cane that smokes
neon-pink in the sunset of dusk.

Here, distances are Siberian. Steppe on steppe
of stars turn out: noctilucent in the blue-black
skin of night. Bright as postage stamps,

the lorikeets play tag from tree to tree,
merry in Regency green. Contemporary.
On Kelly's beach, crooked as English teeth,

the black rocks copy sentinels, and stand
aboriginal against Caucasian sand -
light as Chardonnay !

In the pool at the Las Palmas motel
(early '50s, Festival of Britain style).
we swim under shooting stars, and think of

sacerdotal Chekhov. Toughing it out on Sakhalin.

My Great Grand-Parents

came from North London,
but lived poles apart.
She, with her quartet and baby grand.
He, a registrar for British Rail,
laid tracks across Russia,
but died in snow-bound Odessa,
like a character out of Conrad.

Fading Fast

Around me my ancestors
are grouped in sepia-tinted pose -
a photo of music teachers in decline.
Taken in the 1890s:
you can tell by the clothes.

Their faces - a jolly lot - are kind.
My great-grandmother, in bombazine,
looks resigned;
I think I have her nose.
sits by her husband
in repose,
with family in front and behind.

Out in the garden: *alfresco*
under trees, a little girl -
my grandma - sits on her knees.
Ingenuously she directs her gaze
among the uncles, cousins, aunts,
into the camera, and shyly smiles:
unusual for those days.

On Reconciliation

Our meeting, by a field of grass, soon passed,
and all the ironies I learned too late
were cast, across old books and Norfolk sand:
you said if love should fail to recreate
the peaceful past, describe our loving state
when first we met, were endless rhyme,
then let this language cancel out all crime
of joint neglect; the seasons in the shade:
with words and song we'll let unwind
those inner clocks of silence that we made;
for now we find, within this meeting, brief,
a chance to unlock time, forgetting grief.

Amorino

My late winter child,
sweet as a snowdrop,
was born in a hospital full of women.
Hampstead on his birth certificate:
no father's name given.

*It's 1973 and the country's strike-ridden,
hospital beds with paper sheets,
they put us out on the streets...*

My longed-for son,
perfect little boy,
plump as a *putto*, a week overdue,
no wrinkled skin for you!
I wrap you in pastels, kiss
your silver crown of hair.

*There's an oil crisis; the country's bankrupt,
calling for IMF loans ...*

Friends bring flowers
to welcome my bright-eyed,
long-limbed boy. I hold you close:
this is peace, ecstasy, joy.
I take you home. Alone.
Our journey together has begun.

Auden's Autograph

About love, he was never wrong.
Packed tight as a strudel,
his heart finally gave in,
layer on layer of pain choking him.
About truth, he was always right,
tabling it, and keeping lists.
About time,he was punctilious.
Fastidious. Towards the end,
I met him. Carpet-slippered,
he walked on stage at one of those
late Sixties *literaryfests*. In a crumpled suit,
he stopped us all in our tracks, and wrote
again and again, his autograph for us,
in his small, neat, meticulous hand.

Mr Greenwood at the V&A

I saw him sleeping:
old egret's head,
balding like a cheap pearl.

Shedding his skin,
in this Civil Service
office, with its light film
of library dust,

a grotto of cracked enamel,
where paper-keepers,
mill tea like rust

and lift leather-bound volumes
aloft into the dark vaults
of shelves, glorious as notes
from shiny organ pipes.

Old brain, tabled like a ledger,
remembers youth
on Clapham Common

scenting the stampede
of summer
with his blood-orange nose,

so that I would dearly
have taken him from this place
and led him, like a pit-pony
to pasture.

Half-Term

They come in drenched with rain
or from some unspeakable game
into this grey-walled classroom
with the greyer light outside,
speaking Cantonese or Mandarin,
complaining about tights stolen
or mislaid, these Chinese girls I teach.
At night, they cry under their duvets
of brightly-coloured Tiggers and Pooh Bears,
long for Taiwan, Hong Kong, and Shanghai,
escape from brutal England; the execrable food.

Half-term offers some respite; a landlady's gain.
And all the time. This rain.

The Chinese Rock Garden

The model was part of a gift sent by Chia Ch'ing (Emperor of China 1769-1820) to Josephine, wife of Napoleon Bonaparte. The ship, bringing the gift, was captured by an English man-of-war.

Flawed by the repetition of rain, the museum
boasts red brick and theatrical iron-work.

I walk to Bethnal Green, where under glass,
the garden is all sea-salt and lead paint

shrunk to the size of thimbles and verdigris.
Here, kingfisher feathers appal with shape,

the pastes are ground from mercury.
decorated with coral and shell,

a bridge crosses the great Wall of Pearl.
Wharfed in pavilions, away from the sea,

cluster lantern enamels and ivory:
small buds of metal bent on alchemy.

Cheap Thrills

Without putting a name to this feeling,
I get up, and sit by my window,
knowing the day will not improve,
and the harsh November light
won't lift.

I approve. This is the washed-out
winter sky I want. Sparse leaves
- love notes pinned to a tree -
pleas for mercy, like those votives
left in Spanish chapels: billet-doux
to God; photos of painted, plastic saints:
aide-mèmoires to love.

In the Hotel Wilson, Ghent

Now, with my back to Europe,
I can see across wide vistas
and the mortal streets,
a ragged route lead out
from this dark place,
to where the grey meets
sky and sea.

This evening, by the table's lamp
I write about the mystery
of cobbled towns, and see
the traffic stop outside:
a poor, tired heart,whose
red light bleeds
to death.

Would I had eyes to see
beyond the vision
of this world. The table-tops
remind of money-lending
centuries of coin. Behind
thin walls the lovers
close their blinds.

I have a pack of cigarettes
called *Life*. I light the last:
no one is here to share
this irony with me.
The waiter brings the bill
and takes the plates
- indifferently.

I stay, count the sugar cubes
and watch night fall,
across the dark canals,
where stony birds drop down
upon the crenellations of the town,
and far away recall my only exit
to the sea.

Three Castles

Newly-met, we visited Warwick castle.
Remember, love, then, we had ramparts
around us, and tall stone walls,
too high to climb. But, we tried,
and stepped, blinking, into bright sunlight
to have our first photo taken together,
near a passage carved out of solid rock.
Next, Lewes. I followed you, map in hand,
through the mighty barbican,
up spirally staircases, to view
the safety of open countryside around us.
A couple now, we shared the same guide book.
Finally, Bodiam. Our last castle. Moated.
In deep water now: you liked the armour;
I, the heraldry. This time, we posed behind
dark glasses, smiled, walked the battlements;
took *National Trust* tea, and stood
hand in hand, by a long line of trees.

Freeway

If, while driving across America, in an old pick-up
with only a handful of stars sifted
onto the dark, urban sky, you pause to think of me,
in an Edwardian seaside town, perhaps, or slicing
glistening, emerald kiwi sundials for my tea,
smile, beloved, above the quiet hum of the engine,
at those memories of white-washed cliffs; frilly
English tea-shops. Flinty fossil collections. Me.

Night Vision

I want to go back
to that first meeting
with you (in your tuxedo)
and me,with my heart already
gift-wrapped for you, in my
red dress from *Oasis.*

I want to to return
to that ballroom
in a hotel in a northern city
and watch you, vulpine and adept
circle the room, looking
for young flesh.

I want to sit here
with a beer in my hand,
on this my opening night, my debut,
practising the lines I intend
to speak to you, as my eyes
follow you.

I want to remember
the miracle of your walking
towards me, your hesitant smile,
and hear your cautious script:
native wit; your *idiolect*
as you talk to me.

I want to hold you
out on that dance floor,
a man picked from an identity parade,
with the pine scent of your body
and sleek hair, and the way
you keep me at arm's length.

I want.

The Purple Cortina

The man in the house across the road
makes love to his girl all night,
in front of his rented telly,
and under a naked light.

He drives a purple Cortina,
automatic - GXL -
and works in a white goods' store,
where they recondition and sell.

Their room is like a filmscreen:
their bodies light up the space,
as I watch from my bedroom window,
behind the arcane lace

and drink to their fine love-making,
which takes me back to a golden age,
as I close my velvet curtains
in front of their garish stage.

Interior Scene

Not a picture on the wall
not a book in sight
just a plant in a corner
pleading for light.

You give me back my belongings
you take back the love you gave
you hand me the money for the taxi
you turn your back and wave.

End of the Road

Blue sky trailing white clouds
like an air display. Trans-coastal,
you drive from New York to L.A.
- a midlife, millennial castaway.
I think of you. Malibu.
Pacific Highway. Rented car.
In motels with a pretty tart;
me in the backseat of your heart.

Seaview

The apartment, three storeys up
is home to us both. We love
its pretence at *International Style:*
light-box-cube-meets-urban
loft-living on the cheap.

A window; floor-length
has a front-seat, high-definition view
of seagulls; life-size, belly-up,
veering off into flight
over rooftops, a yucca and a cherry tree
towards a sparkling lozenge of sea-
layered; stacked like a terrine:
navy, ochre and ultramarine.

At night, the Christmas fairy lights
of red, yellow and green garland
The New Kemp Town Brewery:
a hansel-and-gretel house -
toast-warm; cheery,
as we both stare down
from our grey-brick '70s -inspired *chic*
at the NO ENTRY sign, in white.

White as the shimmering, southern light.

Lost at Sea

Let me decipher your body's alphabet,
the perfect H of frame and limbs
and eyes of mid-Atlantic grey
that pull me down to the deep sea-bed
of gasping, air-less longing to escape.
Like the pages of unopened *Vogue,*
your body smells of innocence and crime -
narcotics rushing to the brain,
a poisoned perfume in between the lines.
I read the words: the cuneiform
of brow and hair. Your mouth
that spells out cruelty and despair.

I place you in the context of the sea:
a backdrop to the sky and pebbled shore,
so pull me further to the fathoms deep,
until the letters blur and lose their shape.

Andromeda's Rock

Like this shifting sea here
my love for you
rocks to and fro,
between acceptance
and letting go.

Doomed and irreconcilable, and
bound my heart and soul to you,
I rise on your currents
and go down
on the undertow,
fearful of drowning, so clinging
and not knowing how far out to go.

Free for You

The warm sunshine of New Year's Day
brings the men out: recalescent
in their jeans and perfect hair:
a black-leathered *passeggiata*
past the benches and the lobster claw
of Granada's giant earth-mover for
'Operation Seaclean' on the shore.

Each archway shelters drunks
and shivering boys for rent,
as I walk along this esplanade -
a testament to urban pride. Well-meant.
Built by Kendall, *circa* 1828, bordering
Busby's palatial estates...
Now, dogs pee against graffitied walls:
escutcheoned cock and a pair of balls!

Free for you: coupons, chips with every meal.
A gift with every purchase made before
the first of the second, ninety-four.
Love on offer. Red hot pokers in the grass.
Ships out at sea, and the men who pass.

Without Your Valentine

my life has dimmed.
I droop like a snowdrop
in February -
the month of funerals.

That jacuzzi of emotions,
love, has stilled.
No rain-bruised roses
at my door.
No heart-red envelope
of hope.
No chocolates filled
to bursting point!

No matter I'm all alone;
there's always your voice
on the answerphone.

Without Him

You fill your life with booze
and buy new shoes
get into debt
and read Collette
but nothing fits without him.

You say a prayer
and cut your hair
sleep all you can
with any man
but nothing's fun without him.

Day in, day out,
that endless pain
won't go away without him.
Until one day you start to like
your life without him.

Shock Treatment

Always wash your hands
before writing a poem.
(You don't have to make beds
to dream in them),
but clean hands are needed
for poems.

In homes, women
scrub their hands
until they bleed.

Your methods may be less
extreme. But remember
rich lathers always leave
the towel clean.

This is the way to end dirt,
to deodorize skin
to emulsify dreams, to know

that in institutions you're mad
if you go more than skin deep.

The Ophelia Syndrome

Oh girls, married or unwed,
making dinner, night after night,
for Mr Not-Quite-Right,
and allowing him into your bed.
Staying for the children,
loving your children,
spare a thought for poor Ophelia.
Dead. Sent mad, quite mad.
Covered in pansies and columbine, too,
don't let it happen to you.

Not the Girl I Was

Maybe I lack character,
or was I just *mal élevé*,
but I can't help feeling I've changed
much since yesterday. At 18,
in my duffel coat with its CND badge,
I went on marches. Joined Amnesty.
Campaigned for Civil Rights - passionately.
Now, middle-aged, I know the score,
long in the tooth, nothing shocks any more,
just greed and venality around me,
the shocking British hatred of success;
schadenfreude at anyone's bad luck.
In this country it was ever thus.
My values haven't quite gone, though
tinged with cynicism and regret.
I may be beaten. I'm not out yet.

The Burghers of Calais

A fashionable sextet are they,
the *Burghers of Calais,*

Place a white-boned skull
among their forms,
and watch the bronze at play.

These Rodin made, and placed
en plein air, where
the water at Millbank

flows in its chains
and passes the hostages there.

Eustache, Jean d'Aire
do you know, or care

that the war-lords remain,
la nature humaine
hasn't changed.

That these people who stand
back and stare are the same?

The Sand-pit at Notre-Dame, Paris

a modern nursery rhyme

The children come here gleefully
in their twos and threes
to play the games they've learned
in different nurseries.

Here's the little mongol girl
let's stand and simply stare
and, if the game is interesting,
pretend she isn't there.

Look! The child who's deaf and dumb.
is playing in the sand,
he doesn't know we're teasing him,
he doesn't understand.

The bourgeois couple over there
are very *comme il faut*,
they buy their children everything,
and want us all to know.

The little girl with the big club-foot,
is taunted by her nurse:
'You're not like other children'
is her stupid, mindless curse,

I don't want to stay here,
and see the children fight,
so close the gates securely,

and we'll all go home for the
night.

A Short Story

Today I took two children
to the *Place des Vosges*.
They ate *glaces* by the fountain,
hosed by the light spray...

Here, Mme. de Sevigné
once entertained Corneille
Now, pruned trees shade
this urban everglade.

A child is playing in the sand,
exploring sunlight with his hand.

Change

The thin woman in *Alldays*
is dead. Cancer they said.
She never smiled
when she took the customers' money,
handling their change like a loaded gun.
She was quite young,
often changed her hair colour
and didn't like men.

The Secret is Out

Spring 1999

The hot spotlight of spring
glares down on us all,
with its daffodil-yellow stare.

This green eruption
hurts worse than winter,
scares like stage-fright -
thrusts us all centre-stage.

Big, bronze fields
peeled into segments,
are stripped and seeded,
while the gulls,
flutter like white origami above,
and lambs, in this fresh greenness play,
among the lace trimmings of snowdrops,
and crocus and all those delicate pink blossoms,
as bombs fall over Kosovo.

Better a Dinner of Herbs
Where Love Is

Scholars discuss whether Osman struck coins,
as the solid gold waitress hands out the chips.

Kingly, the watercress joins every dish, for
the white plates are heavily waiting for tips.

Melon-cool blondes let the loving cups tilt
for their lovers to savour the shape of their lips

and the menus stand up for the starved world to see
how greedily we eat up these words *sans-souci.*

The Norwich Floods, 1878

Effluent from the river
courses downstream:
Dies Irae calls a kingfisher:
stained glass on the fields.

There once stood a heronry
in this medieval forest,
lost and gone forever
when the city caved in.

Did you see the water rising
over Lakenham it came
furled by the rivers' join
pumping water to its groin.

Canaries dead in cages
drowned like buddhas
stiff with prayer; plagues of Egypt
covered fields of level grey.

And people shone their flares, with eyes
that watched a Venice improvised.

Turner at Petworth

From the terrace, Turner painted
pale escarpments made of stone,
as the deer pace gently lakewards,
noses stuffed with white limestone.

Baroque trophies litter walkways
- congeries of stones and oaks -
Ducks skim contoured water,
caught in endless parallax ...

Past the ornamental features:
full, patrician, over-blown
catching sight of fallen chestnuts,
we watch the sunset's 'coloured light.'

55th Wedding Anniversary

Powys, Wales

We walk to your cottage gate,
hesitate to enter where
brave phlox and sweet peas
welcome us, (that rambler
round the dog-pawed door)
opening to the flag-stoned floor.

Two good old souls,
you sit like Toby jugs,
shiny with country health.
Your thoughts the tick-tock
of the clock given before
so many interludes of war.

We toast to celebrate.
The sherry burns my throat.
We congratulate you both in turn.
A couple made to sculpt in stone,
yet warm, made of human clay.
The strength of time and love alone.

The Shape of Clouds

In 1803, Luke Howard devised a scheme
for the classification of cloud types.

Before you,
I never noticed the shape of clouds,
how they can float in pairs,
across the sky.

Before you,
no such shapes existed, only
luminous pillows and foamy quilts,
that let the blue
show through.

before you.

A Restoration Tragedy

homage to Sir George Gilbert Scott.

In Westminster Abbey, the vergers deliberate,
walled in by stone, and sealed off like saints,
closely resembling those martyrs: Scott's surfeit
of slap-happy chevrons in heavy lead paint.
In prismatic chapels, incandescence reflects
a sham *Mittelalter,* that's recent and feint,
so the glow of the old king's round circlet, backdates
to a time that was courtly: a blue firmament.
Though the colours run freely, polychromy grates,
for it's fake medieval, though blended with tints
of fine gold, racy lapis: enough's adequate
to gild up God's lily, and cover up hints
that all's not well, and the bodies of men,
are right to be covered, like abbeys, with stone.

Why Weymouth?

Sometimes the need
to get on a train
becomes so great
I find myself in Swanage or Ramsgate
for goodness' sake, among
Saturday afternoon shoppers
wondering why I'm here.
I just had to get away.
For a day. With my books, you see.
I'll go anywhere for a good, long read.

Thank You for Having Me

I've been on this planet,
dear Mother Earth
for fifty-five years,
as a privileged guest
of your generosity.
Tried my best
not to make a mess.
Gave up the car,
walked, cycled everywhere.
Recycled. Not enough.
Although I'll never fully grasp
Quantum mechanics, or the wave
theory of electrons, I know
we're all fleshed together in a chain
of being - kastri.
Even the nasty
are catalysts, propelling us forward.
From bad, the plain good can grow.
Around us
spirits of the loved guide
and protect us. Morphic resonance;
we're all in this dance
as mere heartbeats, inconsequential ciphers
clichéd infinitesimal grains of sand
as these 3.9 billion years began.
Good to others is the only creed;
kindness the true religion.
Here, in the sated West

I suppose we're blessed. I should've
done more
to help the poor, the dispossessed.
Did my modest best.

Late Show at the West Pier

Like lifting the lid of a tureen,
or watching icons of the silver screen,
these starlings rise and skim, locust-like,
above the West Pier's domes, and flying low,
blacken, with shadows, the sun-scorched stones.

Motel

The bathroom's pure Hollywood:
faux-marble, strip-lighting -
mirrors everywhere. The carpets
smell of rain-washed dog; mauve
polyester's on the bed. What's more,
leaves of unknown trees
are lapping outside my door.

Crystal Gazing

You say you love this time of the day,
with the pier sparkling like a starlet
watching her reflection in the sea,
so you hold on to me, in the corner
of this room: bow-fronted, with a balcony.

Like a votary, I've offered candles, relics, charms
for your presence here with me,
at this window, with an oblique view of the sea.

Fallen Idols

For Robert Pépin

Elvis Presley, you taught me
what sex was, when I was ten,
and didn't know anything then.
But that raw ache remained
in my brain, awakened,
but never explained.

Jacques Brel, your songs
of pain, when I was eighteen,
warned that love wasn't sweet.
Wallace Stevens, you opened
a box so bright, the colours were right
and the light, it was dazzling.

Joni Mitchell, so bitter-sweet,
living your life from week to week.
Counting and singing in time.
You got straight to my heart,
acted the part. Said it all before.
So why must I live it all now?

Mid-July

A weak weather front
has eclipsed the sun
this summer,
sent it running for cover
behind clouds,
plush as a cushioned car.
It's rained for weeks.
Some days,
brief, ambient sunlight
sends out fretful patrols
onto the city streets.

The Appropriate Country

Everyone has a spiritual home -
a sense of place. Sanctuaries
for their restlessness. There's
higher ground to discover -
a lifetime's quest.

I wish I could close the wide water,
full circle, with an arm's embrace
and make the parting less.

Thanks to Sonja Ctvrtecka, Judy Anderson &
Simon Jenner for funding this volume.

Tristan Green Design

Suite 4   50 Grand Parade   Brighton   East Sussex   BN2 2QA
T/F: 01273 602988   M: 07980 271563
E: tristan.green@virgin.net